W9-AUI-509

THE UNSTILL ONES

PRINCETON SERIES OF CONTEMPORARY POETS

Susan Stewart, *series editor*

For other titles in the Princeton Series of Contemporary Poets see page 79

THE UNSTILL ONES

Poems

Miller Oberman

PRINCETON UNIVERSITY PRESS
Princeton & Oxford

Copyright © 2017 by Princeton University Press

Published by Princeton University Press, 41 William Street,
    Princeton, New Jersey 08540
In the United Kingdom: Princeton University Press, 6 Oxford Street,
    Woodstock, Oxfordshire OX20 1TR

press.princeton.edu

Cover image: Page from the *Exeter Book* / Exeter Cathedral Library.
    Reproduced with the permission of Bernard J. Muir.

All Rights Reserved

ISBN 978-0-691-17682-6

ISBN (pbk.) 978-0-691-17683-3

Library of Congress Control Number: 2016960846

British Library Cataloging-in-Publication Data is available

This book has been composed in Adobe Garamond Pro, ScalaSans OT and Norse

Printed on acid-free paper. ∞

Printed in the United States of America

10 9 8 7 6 5 4 3 2 1

Contents

ᛗ

ᛏ

NIGHT WATCH

He was riding in the dark
            down a burned mountain.
      Nothing grew here,
                  jagged crags of stone,
                        hacked hunks of old wayposts,
            the sky charred to a gray coal.

It was always night.
            He was chasing something.
      He was running from something.
                  His horse flung his legs out and rowed at the rocks.
                        Fling out, row back, fling out, row back.
            He had been on the horse so long

he felt welded to it,
            he could feel the stones jutting into its hooves
      as if his arms had grown down the beast's
            arms, until his hands
                  were wrapped around hooves.
            They swooped down, fell down, charged

down, and the loose cinders shifted.
            They saw nothing else alive. Not
      a crow. Not a mouse or earthworm.
                  His horse was so flat out he could feel his own
                        face hovering an inch above the ground.
            His face and Supernatural's face, that was

the horse's name, grimed in dark dust.
            He was remembering about water, drinking it.
      He was remembering the old book,
                  pages fine and crisp as onion skin,

where he'd read *Supernatural* was "a force
above nature. From medieval Latin.

Supernatural things, *now rare*." Rare,
     the riches of a language kept in books,
   words and more words to describe those.
          Family trees of words, their heirlooms,
               their family jewels. His own jewels
          ached, riding from ruin to ruin.

Horses, he had read, are a joy to the un-still ones.
          The pages turned in him. *Horse*,
     meaning, to run. From the days
          when a thing was what it did,
               the act of naming itself a desire
          for stillness, for containment.

THE UNSTILL ONES

CÆDMON'S HYMN

[translated from the Old English]

Now we will honor the heaven-kingdom's keeper,
the measurer's might, and his mindthoughts,
the work of the wonder father, as he wrought,
boundless lord, the beginning of every beauty.
The first poet made, for the souls of soil,
heaven for a roof, holy maker.
After that, mankind's keeper made
middle-earth, master almighty,
eternal lord, earth, for everyone.

ON TRANS

The process of through is ongoing.

The earth doesn't seem to move, but sometimes we fall
down against it and seem to briefly alight on its turning.

We were just going. I was just leaving,
          which is to say, coming
elsewhere. Transient. I was going as I came, the words
          move through my limbs, lungs,   mouth, as I appear to sit

peacefully at your hearth   transubstantiating some wine.
          It was a rough red,   it was one of those nights we were not
forced by circumstances   to drink wine out of mugs.
Circumstances being, in those cases, no one had been

transfixed at the kitchen sink long enough   to wash dishes.
          I brought armfuls of wood   from the splitting stump.
Many of them, because it was cold,   went right on top
          of their recent ancestors.   It was an ice night.

They transpired visibly,   resin to spark,
          bark to smoke, wood to ash.   I was
transgendering and drinking   the rough red at roughly
          the same rate   and everyone who looked, saw.

The translucence of flames   beat against the air
          against our skins.   This can be done with
or without clothes on.   This can be done with
          or without wine or whiskey   but never without water:

evaporation is also ongoing.   Most visibly in this case
        in the form of wisps of steam   rising from the just washed
            hair
of a form at the fire whose beauty was   in the earth's
        turning, that night and many nights,   transcendent.

I felt heat changing me.   The word for this is
        transdesire, but in extreme cases   we call it *transdire*
or when this heat becomes your maker we say
        transire, or when it happens   in front of a hearth:

transfire.

WULF AND EADWACER

[after the anonymous Old English poem of the same title]

The poem is either about a woman
separated from a man by a petty
tribal war, or about a woman
forced to live with a second man
because of a petty tribal war.
Either way, she bears a child.
Either way, one man is kept
prisoner on an island, guarded
by bloodthirsty swords. Either
way, the woman sits crying
in the rain, sheltered by trees,
or it could be the rain is crying,
or it could be there is no rain,
she's only using it as an image.

The second man, who is not
the island prisoner, whose name
means possession-watcher,
comes to the woman to protect
her, or imprison her, or because
he wants a woman just then,
and so fucks her. This feels good
to her because she's lonely, or
likes a good fuck sometimes,
or because she loves this second
man, not the first. But afterwards
it sickens her, out of loyalty
to the imprisoned man, or because
the second man seemed pleasing
at first, but then less so.

The child is sent to the woods
to die or kill or escape with the
island man, who may have got
free of the bloodthirsty men
or stuck them with their own
swords. Then there is either
an eagle or a cruelty, or cruelty
to the woman has always seemed
inseparable from eagles, or the
one who copied her poem
suffered from partial blindness
and wrote the wrong word
entirely. Certainly sharp-edged
things, carnage, slaughter. Or
the island was only an image,
and there was never an island,
she only meant we seemed so
distant from each other we might
as well be on two islands separated
by a hard salted sea, and neither
of us ship builders. In this case
there were no islands, men, or
swords, but instead a hopeless
separateness ending in a wood
full of wolves or a man called
Wulf, and though she has known
hunger, it is not hunger that carves
her belly with dread but longing
for a man, or child, or wolf
because *it is easy to separate that*
which has never been joined, meaning
the second man has no true claim
on her, or the first, or the life
of the child in the woods
is worth less than the frost
of breath hanging briefly
on a cold night, soon eaten
by the cold.

And when it disappears
who is to say then what it meant,
what form it had, whose mouth
released it thoughtlessly, or
perhaps looked at it and knew
how small a time its form
would hold against the night.

ALOUD, OUT OF NOTHING

Alone I am driven each day before daybreak
        toward the shadow-side of the rocks.
I sing of times trans-shifting, and I write
        here at the quiet limit of the world
whose tongue gave gold to the language.

It was my own, own body I saw,
        I look so raw and unfinished,
hanging from rafter and groined roof
        that hardly hold it safely.

I am not dead in my sleep.
        The nightbuds were too strangely still,
even the windflowers lay flat,
        the fields had other business at that hour.

Do things still matter? They matter.
        Close your eyes, change horses.
Time was. Time was,
        within the riding,

a way to measure out the wind.
        And in my hands this crust.
I blow on the live coal. I would be the one.
        I know I am through with cleverness, I know—

What people do, an honest tongue can talk about.

THE CITY

Was a ruin even
before it was a ruin.
Up-dug its boneyards,
made them parks,
moved the stones out
and moved the stones
out again, took louder
neighbors who danced,
who drilled down.
Sunk pipes, fitted them
to other pipes, filled them
with rivers, drunk
from the rivers, said
no water was ever
sweeter, no flowers
lusher, no fires burned
longer. Oily ash collected
on our fan blades,
sills, in our shoes
if we left them out.
Everything dusted
with our own dead
matter. We held it
in our mouths, slept
under its covers. We
moved the graves
beyond the gates,
past the curved iron,
curved stone.

THE RUIN

[translated from the Old English]

Wondrous is this wall-stone, broken by fate,
the city burst apart, the giant-work crumbled.
Roofs are ruined, towers ruined,
rafters ripped away, hoarfrost on lime,
gaps in the storm-shelter, sheared and cut away,
under-eaten by age. The earth grip holds
the mighty makers, decayed and lost to time,
held in the hard-gripping ground while a hundred generations
of people watched, then died. Often this wall waited,
lichen-gray and red-stained, through one kingdom after another,
stood against storms until steep, deep, it failed.
Yet even now the [   ] heaped over with [   ]
remains [   ]
savagely scraped [   ]
grimly ground up [   ]
[   ] shone [   ]
[   ] skillful work ancient building [   ]
[   ]g [   ] earth-rind bent
the mind [   ] swift motion
the mind-renowned one bound up in firm rings,
house walls, wonderfully, with wire strips.
Bright were the fort-buildings, bathhouses,
a wealth of high gables, much martial sound,
many meadhalls full with joy-days
until the force of fate turned that.
Bodies died all over the place in battle, days of pestilence came,
death swept away all of the sword-brave men.
This came to be their strife-place, their waste-places,
their battle places became blasted waste,
the fort-place rotted apart. The repairers died,

armies to the earth. For that reason these houses are failing,
the red expanses, the open places and shelters,
and the woodwork of the roof. The place of ruin fell,
broken to mounds where once many men,
mood-glad and gold-bright, clothed in gleaming,
gold-adorned and wine-flushed, war-gear shining,
and looked on treasure, silver, curious gems
on property, on lands, on jewel-stones,
on this bright city, this broad realm.
The stone halls stood, the hot stream gushed
in a wide billow, and a wall held all of it
in its bright breast, and that bath was
hot in its heart. That was fitting.
Then they let flow [   ]
hot streams over old stone
[   ]
[   ] until the ringed pool hotly [ ]
[   ] where they were.
When is [   ]
[   ] That is a kingly thing
house [   ]
        [   ] city [   ]

THE SMOKEWOOD TREE

The smokewood tree dropped its leaves
in our hands and we sewed them
into living cups. We drank until
the leaves weathered, went shattery
against our lips. We used our lips
for many things, talking, singing,
lovemaking, except in the silent
season, which was for harvest
and contemplation when we
forbid ourselves speech
and sealed ourselves
tight as the blue smokewood bark
which holds to its trunk
with a layer of sap. In that sap
the night-flies hatch, and we let
our thoughts do the same, but
as for me, the silent season
is hard. It is blue out,
the blue is full of chattering
branches, their voices
covered not in moss, but
frost. Frost. Like a fur hood
I can't fling back against my shoulders.

TABULA RASA

One day it rained. One day a green
inchworm crawled along his hand.
One night they held his head as he drank
sharp-root wine from the fossilized cup.
His mother, grandmother, and her older
sister, knuckles bulky as oak-burls.
His mother, who was called *the proud*
in reverence or scorn. He lay on the table
used for nothing except this. This: had
no name, though naming happened here.
The three dipped their quills, etched
the tree's body into his own, roots
reaching down the tender arches of his feet.

He lay silent as they spoke and sang,
worked stories into his skin; trunk and twig.
As ring eternal they rang into him.
One day a musca fly sucked at his ink.
One day he heard the clouds shaking
rain from their pockets, little rains
chiming out like coins falling on stone.
One night vesper thrushes lit in his hair,
tore dark tendrils for their nests,
then winged off as the three worked,
their fingers like fissures he fell into.

GOOD SLEEP

This is nothing
like the times I have been weak,
lead-limbed when they come for me,
unable to move or speak.
These limbs, light as charged copper.

I grin at my army, run alone
at the other, cut them down
with my blade. They ripple
to the ground like gray silk.

The slashed field green-soaked,
their armor green-black,
saturate as an oil painting
under the sun's lamp.

I hack from the hip.
Their heads, un-helmeted, come
to rest in the field, open-mouthed,
relieved, and briefly near my boots.

At the end of the field
I run through the woods,
weave through the branches,
high-horned, fierce as a stag.

No one ever touched me
when I rushed against their lives.
Their lives, which seemed
eager to come to me, so
beautifully did I kill them.

LIES AFTER THE WAR

We went to Bull Run, or was it Manassas,
one of those, past Battlefield Ford, past
Glory Days bar in the strip mall, or
was it before the mall was built, or

was it after the mall was abandoned.
I was grizzled with age, I was
twenty-one, at the small beige
visitor center. I remember it without

sound. They had a machine there that
sucked up sound. It was mostly made
of hollows, blanks, lack, and also
plastic. It came with a smaller version

of itself, whose job was to suck
the sound of the larger sound-
sucker. It did its work. It was about
the size of a foot. Either run that,

or the place would be filled with ordinary
sounds, squirrels twitching their tails,
chattering, one to another in their ceaseless
brag about acorn-hordes. They couldn't risk

the sound of dirt, suffocated under the sewn
sod, or the possibility of rustling leaves.
This is not the grass where it happened,
not the starved pines. These clouds have

shifted. Never do they look like hacked
arms, heaped corpses. We lay in the sound-

empty field under the cloud constellation
of Virginia. Look up: that one's a crutch,

that one's a stump, that one's a burning
town, and the yellow tendrils of gangrene.
The air turned to ether. The ether was
painless, it was all painless, I swear.

THE SKY-STONE

(In the field behind his town   lived the sky-stone.
      One night   he curled around it
curved where it curved   lay in its coolness
     fitted his hips   to the damp place it met the earth.

They said the ground   under the stone
      was like other ground.   They said the stone
had been a star   that came unstuck so long ago
    all the trees it crushed   came back, their twirling

seed-puffs rolled off   the crushed trees,
     rooted, and grew.   They said the stone
was twice as big at first   but wore down
    over time the way windows   are worn soft, beaten away by
     rain).

But no ground   is like other ground

THE WOMAN WHO CANNOT

[translated from the Old English]

*The woman who cannot bring forth her child: go to a dead man's grave
    and then step three times over the grave, and then say these words three
    times:*

This is my cure for the loathsome late-birth
This is my cure for the bitter black-birth
This is my cure for the loathsome imperfect-birth

*And when that woman is with child and she goes to her lord in his bed,
    then let her say:*

Up I go, over you I step,
with a quick child, not a quelled one,
with a full-born one, not a doomed one.

*And when the mother feels the child is quick, go then to a church, and
    when she comes before the altar, say then:*

Christ, I said it. This has been uttered.

*The woman who cannot bring forth her child: grasp a handful of her
    own child's grave, and after that, bind it in black wool and sell it to
    peddlers, and say then:*

I sell it, you sell it.
This blackened wool, this sorrow seed.

MY BROTHER WAS MISSING

Six kids in a warehouse, green arms of trees and the floor covered in
salt for dancing—*it's like oozing on the floor of the sea*, they said,
when the juice evaporated. Who did they say it to? Who quivered?
Have you ever had a dream without yourself in it?

The names for tools had all changed: now you had to hit a nail with a
bangest, and weld with a *blow-flame,* and know the lengths of level
planks with a *slam-box.*

Legs and arms in deep prayer under all the flailing branches in the
galaxy. They flew kites in the ware, they squawked. All veering
inside fire, minds like mazes.

I had no jaw, hands, voice, skin, muscle, no gaze, no silky veins
spread under—only nearness but no sorrow and also no quills, no
swimming because of suns which dried up oceans or which-have-
you when oceans dry up, leaving only crumbs and exiles.

It was now I realized I must stop saying "I," it was become an
addiction and made no sense, but pronouns in general are truly
sordid creatures scuttling about among feet. (Forgot to say "feet"
are called "ribbons" now, ironically.)

List of bans for tonight (who posts it unknown): no stars, no rum, no
window-smashing, no kissing, no squid, no lying on lambskin rugs,
no crying, no voracious guzzling: a pox on junk.

If I am not in the vastness of this sleep-country who is? In the
night someone woke up sweating. Who-knows-who-it-was, the
kids didn't know, they being just foxes without families, no one

watching all those little limbs to see that none go splitting out against the flaming blue moon, none to be awake when they slept to watch so no one goes up-gazed.

All things being equal, they is not.

THE VESPERTINES

1.

Do you remember when we were green and supple
I told you stories, my sapling, my brother-sister,
those nights not-sleeping on our bedrolls
made of boiled wool and moss
and I told you of the cloud-maker, ghost
in the cloud-house who made the night-
white wisps and noon-heavy layers,
who drifted in our door—I translated
for you what the cloud-maker said,
the billowing stories that dissolved you,
once, what was the one, do you
remember, that drifted you, laughing,
to sleep?

2.

We read a book, later, about two
brothers from a far country,
one who died of a cough, the other
soon after in a fire, and both woke, and
both rode to a valley of orange blossoms
and cherry blossoms on a white horse
and found kindness, and found kindness,
and joined the orchard workers' rebellion
against unjust taxes and were killed
in battle by the landowners' arrows—
was that, do you remember, the book
singed so we never knew its ending,
or did they wake up again, elsewhere?

BROTHERS

What are brothers?
Are they two trees, saplings, seeds
dropped near each other, blossoms
pollinated by the same bee or wind?
Do the silver roots twine down,
touch in the soil, drink the rain
that seeps beneath?

Raised under the same trees,
fed from the same bowls
finger-worn from years of use,
the debris of those years
in my cupboard, in his cupboard . . .

Either the day is off kilter, or it's not. Perhaps
everything's falling out as gravity intends.
We were born right next to each other.
Out of the dark warm globe,
heaved into a brighter one.
Hurled into the outer-earth.
Then the stars he sees
are always a little away from mine.

WOLF BROTHER

Today my brother's
ghost rode with me
on a white wolf,
loping along
at my horse's shoulder.

He was faceless
but I'd know that
bone-house anywhere.
Even in this gray waste,
the dust the world left.

It was the time between
night and morning
we used to call dawn,
the stars clinging
to the dark-losing sheet.

I wanted to plead
with him to speak,
to stay, to steal
his wolf's flesh,
wear that fur awhile.

The sun's rim rose
bloody but he
was not of blood-stuff,
and with the stars
he faded, I want to think,
gently.

SILENTIUM

The sun didn't set, but like a fallen rider
the light un-horsed itself, dove shaggy
into the rucked up mud, and we all
walked down the road in one direction,
some in their last leather, some in silk rotted
gray and brown and bent, and when we
measured our steps past a town, even in wind
the bells swayed toneless and tongueless,
clappers unscrewed and melted down,
wrapped around powder, shipped out in boxes,
the bells bound open as dresses wind-filled
then frozen. What is courage? Had we
had it? What can it mean now as the light is pitched
headlong under our legs, we who sewed up
our mouths and do not know how to die?

THE RUIN

[after the anonymous Old English poem of the same title]

Down the cobbles and across the canal
where the sodium lights of illegal houseboats
bob in the current, my compass gets stuck.
There my friend points, and we go to the chalk-marked
door, tug the chain and pulley and roll under the gate.

       Someone dancing, masked, half lady liberty,
half skeleton.
       The steam vents
chug over the musicians wearing nothing
but brass: tubas, trumpets, trombones
blast the crowd. A crush of warriors
stomps the beat, clashing swords, percussive.

       Someone unbuttons their stolen
prison uniform, pulls a chainsaw from between
sweating thighs, starts it, hefts it,
cuts a gaping window to reveal the canal.
We watch the water glow,
toxic.

       Someone's passing around clear spirits
in corked jars. Bitter
as winter berries, it sizzles the tongue.
Like tasting sparks. Like licking a raw stripped
tree.

       Someone with hair made entirely
of peacock feathers starts the generator,

plugs a mic into an amp, and after the electric squeals the cord, rasps
we are here, we are here

We open the cathedrals of our chests and roar. My friend
leans into the wind
blowing through the fresh-cut hole,
eyes round as shields, hawk-gold. We do not have to touch
to touch.

We dance. Hundreds. Thousands.
We shake the night with Peacock
in the slinky dress of shimmering wet tar.
The canal catches fire, trash islands burn like
wicks floating in kerosene.

Some of us have the beaks of hunting birds,
the oiled armor of cockroaches;
what the old book calls
unclean.

We are unclean.
We burn what they build,
make nothing to replace it, dance
in a radioactive bone-joy,

and my friend, born in the seam
of a coal mining town, grins at me
in our ruined city, in magnesium
flare-dust, burned and burning.

RIDDLE 82

[translated from the Old English]

The thing is [   ]
    [   ] is going, giant, swilling
[   ]
skin not made of flesh, feet [   ]
[   ]
shall mark us all [   ].

THE OLD ENGLISH RUNE POEM

[translated from the Old English]

ᚠ (*feoh*)

    Wealth is a comfort   to every man
    yet every man   must divide it mightily
    If he wishes to have   the measurer's mercy

ᚢ (*ur*)

    The ox is steady-hearted   and over-horned
    A fierce and famous beast   it fights with horns
    Glorious moor-stepper   that is a noble creature

ᚦ (*þorn*)

    Thorn is severely sharp   to every soldier
    Its attack is evil   and immensely cruel
    to any man   who lies with it

ᚩ (*os*)

    The mouth is the source   of all speech
    the support of wisdom   and a solace to the wise
    and brings blessedness   and refuge to every nobleman

ᚱ (*rad*)

    Riding is mild for warriors   at their hearthsides
    and strong-bold   for he mounted on the back
    of a mighty horse   over a distance measured in miles

ᚳ (*cen*)

    Torch is to each of the living   told by its flame
    Bright and beaming   it burns most often
    where nobles   rest indoors

ᚷ (*gyfu*)

    A gift is the grace   and praise of men
    and warmth and worthship   to all exiles
    sustenance for him   who is stripped of all else

ᚹ (*wyn*)

 Joy is won by whoever knows little of woe
 sourness or sorrow and who has for himself
 breath and bliss and fullness and a fortified place

ᚻ (*haegl*)

 Hail is the whitest grain it heaves down from heaven's lift
 The wash of wind rolls it and then it turns to water

ᚾ (*nyd*)

 Need is bound in the breast yet nonetheless becomes for the sons
  of men
 a help and healing both if they heed it in time

ᛁ (*is*)

 Ice is over-cold and immeasurably slippery
 It gleams glass-clear most like precious gems
 Or a floor worked over with frost fair upon seeing

ᛄ (*ger*)

 The year is the gladness of men when God
 holy heaven's king has the earth bear
 bright branches for all men both rich and poor

ᛇ (*eoh*)

 Yew is from without an un-smooth tree
 fixed fast in the earth a keeper of fire
 up-raised by its roots a joy to have in one's realm

ᛈ (*peorþ*)

 Peorþ is a game and perpetual source of pealing laughter
 to strong spirited [ ] where warriors sit
 happily together in the beer-hall

ᛉ (*eolx*)

 Elk-sedge is found most often in a fen
 it waxes in water and wounds severely
 burns in the blood of each man's body
 who with his hand takes hold of it

ᛋ (*sigel*)

 The sun for sailors is a symbol of hope

when they row   over the fishes' bath
until the ocean-horse   brings them to land

ᛏ (*tir*)

Tir is one of the tokens   it holds well true
for princes   and stays on course
over the obscurity of night   and it never yields

ᛒ (*beorc*)

The birch tree is free of fruit   yet even still bears
branches without offspring   it is beautiful in its boughs
high of crown   fairly adorned
leaf-sprung   close against the sky's lift

ᛖ (*eh*)

The war horse is a joy   for noblemen and earls
the charger, hoof-proud   there where warriors
wealthy on steeds   exchange speech
and it is always a solace   to the un-still ones

ᛗ (*man*)

Man in mirth   is dear to his kin
yet must every one   betray the other
for that reason   the Lord dooms
that wretched flesh   to be taken by the earth

ᛚ (*lagu*)

The water is to men   seemingly without end
if they dare to   travel on tilting ships
and the sea-waves   terrify them severely
and the surf-steed   heeds not to the bridle

ᛝ (*ing*)

Ing was first   among East Danes
until afterwards   east over the wave
he departed   followed by his wagon
thus the Hard ones   called that hero

ᛟ (eþel)

Home is over-dear   to each man
If he can enjoy there   all which is right and fit
in his dwelling   with blossoming prosperity

ᛗ (dæg)

Day is a dispatch from the divine   dear to men
Lustrous light of the creator   mirth and hope
for the wealthy and unwealthy   and useful to all

ᚪ (ac)

The oak on earth   is food for the flesh
of the children of men   It often fares
over the sea-bird's bath   The sea tests
whether the oak   holds honorably true

ᚫ (æsc)

The ash is over-high   and dear to all men
Stout in its roots   straight and steadfast in its hilt
Although many men   attack it

ᚣ (yr)

The bow is for nobles   and princes everywhere
joy and honor   and is beautiful on a steed
a piece of war-gear   steady on a far journey

ᛡ (iar)

Iar is a river-fish   yet it enjoys
its food on land   It has a fair home
be-tossed with water   where it lives in joy

ᛠ (ear)

The earth is hideous   to all noble men
when steadily   the flesh begins
to cool   The corpse   the pale one
chooses earth as its bedfellow   Blossoms fall
joys depart   friendship's bonds are broken

THE UNMAKING

At the winter fires
        they used to tell

that come the unmaking
        houses would slowly

at the speed of trees
        growing, ungrow

become trees again
        untimbered.

And baked bread
        become grain

then wheat, then seed.
        Likewise, glass burn

back to sand, sand
        to shells, stones.

Everything wound
        would unwind, shot

sink to ore, drawn
        deep in the ground.

If your voice is the one
        still running clear

when the sun comes up
        the listeners undress you

lift you on their shoulders
        pour you in a sea soak.

Then all you recalled, singing,
        is called back to salt.

Not lost, but unlost,
        absorbed in skin,

skin-riveted, then sloughed
        off again, in time.

ROCKS

There were rocks. Huge, looming,
scored with caves, lunar. It was windy.
He pressed himself into a shallow
depression to light a candle
for his father, as was custom.
The sinking brief flare of the match
three times snuffed out, when,
sulfur-nosed, he lights the small
white candle in its jelly glass.
Makes a cave, hunching
of his body. Makes a cave,
diving, of his mind, singing
into the wind, bent
over the flame. The sun sunk,
the sky a fading blue, deep
violet. He can taste them,
violets, his body a yawn,
a gaping openness arcing
around the memory candle.

A black sliver of wick
drops into the wax pool.
The wind drinks the sound
in a long gulp. The wind
gets so thirsty. All that
blowing.

THE GRAVE

[translated from the Old English]

There was a house built before you were born.
Before you came from your mother, your dust was here.
But it wasn't active, its deepness not known,
not yet locked in what length it would lay for you.

Now you are brought there where you shall be.
Now you are measured, and the dirt after that.

No, your house is not made high with boards,
it is un-high, low when you lie in there.
The cover-walls are low, the side-walls un-high,
the roof is built full near your breast.

So you shall dwell in full-cold soil,
dim and dark. That den fouls around your hands,
that house is doorless and dark within.
There you are kept fast, and death has the key.
That earth-heave is burdensome, and bitter to abide in.

There you shall dwell and worms will dismember you.
There you are laid, and loathsome to your loved ones.
No one, never will a friend come near to see how you are,
to look and see how you like that house,
that will ever undo that door after you
and make light [   ]

For soon you are burdensome and loathsome to see.
(For soon your head is bereft of hair,
all the fairness of your hair is scattered,
and never, no one will stroke it softly with their fingers.)

ON FISHING

There was too much of my father last night.
He kept me, through every brown hour,
awake. Usually my fear is forgetting him.
His particulars. His expressions. Afraid
of his face becoming a statue. But last
night I said stop that. Stop being so
realistic, reminding me you were only
eight years older than I am now when
your heart fisted itself in the kitchen.

We were making peach butter.
There is too much kitchen now.
Too many pots and carrots and tiles.
The stovetop with electric burners
he used to flick ground coffee on,
so I could watch it flare.
Now it's flaring again.
I wish it would stop.
He stopped short as a line
caught in a fish's cheek.
There are too many fish now.
My bed is full of scales and blood,
sinkers and bobbers and boats.

All that tackle in my sheets
is distraction from fear.
Dumb fish, I'm
swimming at the lure.
How embarrassing
to be a person.
Afraid to die.
Afraid to sleep.

I used to sleep in my clothes.
He forbid it. I said why.
He said you cannot sleep in your clothes.
I said why.
He said you cannot sleep in your clothes.
I said why.
He said it's just not done.
That's all.
He didn't know why.
We fought many nights
on the stairs.
He was kind, I see that now,
not to say sleeping
in your clothes
will not make you ready.

AGAINST A SUDDEN STITCH

*Against a sudden stitch, feverfew, and the red nettle that grows
through houses, and waybread. Boil in butter.*

They were loud, oh, loud, when they rode over the hollow,
they were one-minded when they rode over the land.
Shield yourself now to survive this attack.
Out, little spear, if you are in here.
I stood under linden, under a light shield,
where the mighty women take strength by treachery
and shrieking. They send spears.
I will send another after them,
a barb flying forward against them.
Out, little spear, if you are hidden in here.
A smith sat and struck a little sword
made strangely strong with iron.
Out, little spear, if you are in here.
Six smiths sat, working the slaughtering-spears,
out spear, not in, spear.
If there is any amount of iron in here,
any witches' work, it will melt.
If you were shot in hide, or were shot in flesh,
or were shot in the blood
or were shot in a limb, your life will never be lost.
If it was the shot of gods, or the shot of elves
or if it was the shot of witches, now I will help you.
This cures the god's shot, this cures the elf's shot,
this cures the witches' shot, I will help you.
Fly there [   ] to the mountainhead,
be healed, may your lord help you.
Then take that sword, set it in the soak.

NATURAL HISTORY

I wanted to see Comanche,
so you took me in the snow,
to the dusty small-town museum.

You said it had once been fine,
glamorous, even, and the shaggy
Kodiak in the Americas could light

the scene with his teeth. Now
the sky is faded white, water-
stained, paint flakes on the heads

of bobcats and badgers, someone's
tusk fell in the dried-up river,
there's dryrot in the buffalo herd.

Past the desert and beyond
the snowy waste and boreal forest,
in a small black-painted hallway,

there's one glass cube, and in it,
Comanche. He is alone in the cube.
He is not well lit. They have him raised

to a low hover. His hooves dusty
like he just ran in, his coat a claybank shine.
Still saddled and alert, with the kindest eyes.

A man in a trenchcoat shuffles in,
presses himself against the wall
like a moth. I was tired from standing.

My leg hurt. I briefly thought of crying.
I thought of smashing the glass
with a kick, riding Comanche out.

I thought of grabbing your hand,
pulling you into the flat black
paint and kissing you, I thought of

pouring my blood into your blood,
of becoming daylight inside you, of you
becoming the prairie under me, or

above. Of golden grass, of the perfect
darkness behind Comanche,
of the hands that built a wood frame,

cured his hide, stretched it over, and whether
they could recall in their bones what it is
to gallop, flat out, into the streaming—

I thought I wanted to see Comanche
but that was not what I wanted, and
that man was there, in the trenchcoat,

and my shot leg throbbed and I stayed
what I was. A stuffed thing.
I couldn't meet your eyes, only

Comanche's. Which had been
for a hundred years and more, and
continued to be, made out of glass.

THE WORD AGAIN

My friend once didn't thank me
for pointing out five poems in his sheaf
where he'd used the word *pith*. That book
about the never-breaking branch—
dark, in every poem, or nearly. Today

I saw *bear* in mine all over. One with
actual bears, or at least people
resembling bears, galumphing
down the street, and rivers
that bear you up, and then the bearers,
human, of a coffin, but nothing about
what anyone can bear or not bear, nothing
about what can be borne, though there is

one poem skeleton called "Rainbears,"
which are not real and never were.
Shaggyblue, skywater soaked, nothing un-
bearable to them, no sorrow, no rage,
they would be strong as gods.
I was this kind of bear or god, nothing
couldn't be borne, I thought.
No insult, no grief, no binding
lash. When everyone went indoors,
I was dripping fog in the field,
endlessly strong, endlessly crushed. But I'm not,

now, any kind of shabby martyr.
There are unbearable things.
Most things are unbearable.
Being inside when I want to be outside,

interminable fear of doing or saying
the wrong thing, disdain, modernist couches,
many people, not being able to say *this is*—
when it is—*unbearable.*

AGAINST A DWARF

[translated from the Old English]

*Against a dwarf one should take seven little wafers, like those for offering,
    and write these names on each wafer:*

Maximanius, Malchus, Iohannes, Martimanius, Dionisius,
    Constantinus, Serafion.

Then in turn one must sing the spell
that is spoken hereafter. One shall sing, first in
the left ear, then in the right ear, then above that man's
head. And then bring a virgin and hang it around
her neck, and do this for three days. He will soon be better.
In here came a spider-thing,
he held his bridle in his hand, he said that you
                            were his horse,
laid his fetters around your neck. They set
                        to work sailing away from land.
As soon as they came away from land his limbs began to cool.
Then in stalked the beast's sister,
then she ended it and swore oaths
that this could never hurt the sick one
nor the one who obtains the power of this spell
or he who has this spell, speaks this charm. Amen. Fiat.

THE GRAVE

[after the anonymous Old English poem of the same title]

After my father died but
before I died, we sat
at the edge of the sea
in a tall watch chair,
the year the sky changed
its meaning. I was taller,
closer to the world's roof,
or it had fallen an inch
or two, the two inches
my father had that I did not
have, which I now saw,
sitting high off the sand
on the tower made for watching,
in daylight, swimmers.

She had stood at the rim of the woods
the day I lowered his body
gently down with ropes, gently
but not without effort,
the bearers planting their feet
apart, digging in, inverted
sailors, hoisting down not up,
hand over hand, bent forward
not back, hips not opened to sail
and mast but closed. Lowering
a body in a box. In the chair,
not lowered, our two bodies sat
under the sky, two inches
closer, and fell, or continued
falling.

I was not taller, it was the sky
dropped down, and I was I,
pulled back from a yawning
distance into my body. You also
in a body, on the watchpost,
had arms and hands and heat.
The arc of the sky, the illusion
of the sky's arc—came closer.
The stars spread on its blue
curve, and we did not touch
except in the way the sky
touched us, poured its bent
dark down, as if we were
enclosed. Not by a hole
in the earth, but a hole
in self itself, or the illusion that
one person can live inside another.
And if it was not illusion, the sky
came closer, we unburied ones
bore our bones up.

WHO PEOPLE ARE

My mother's people came from France,
from Germany, came from money, came
to New York, to Philadelphia,
went to San Francisco, to Alaska, were
furriers, left us photographs, lithographs,
tintypes of tiny ladies in huge hats,
of bearded gentlemen standing up
straight in Union blue, little girls
in ermine, bear, elk, seal, who sat
in huge chairs with flashing eyes,
who died young. They left us stained
glass windows in synagogues, left
graves off the Jackie Robinson Parkway.

You wanted to be a window washer.
I wanted to ride in horse races
across the desert. We met in the city.
We met in a graveyard. We met
as my father's body was cooling.
Our eyes locked in the yard
as his body was washed and shrouded,
as crockery was shattered, two
blue shards laid over his eyes.

I was nearly a corpse, white-bellied
fish floating down the James.
You were a bear, I was a wolf,
you were a lion, one minute satisfied,
starving the next. I was a mossy place
to kneel on, you were a candle,

you were a singer, I was a river,
I was a soldier, I was a black suit,
you were a black shawl, I was dust
in the sun, you were a window washer.

P. M.

I misread "postmodern" as "postmortem,"
but aren't they both the night of a thing,
post meridiem? There was an even-
ing, this evening, a great evening of
accounts. All the black marks counted up,
tallied, rubbed out, the columns crushed.
Street cleaning, double parking, failure
to stop at a red light, all the meters
swept clean.
             Then it was oysters all
over the place, big as wagon wheels.
A shot of brine for free,
a nickel for a seaweed bed,
a pulsing pillow, a pink jellyfish
flaring its incomprehensible skirts.

RIDDLE 63

[translated from the Old English]

Often I shall say I am beautifully useful
to the hall-joy when I am borne forth
glad with gold, to where men drink.
Sometimes, in the closet, the good servant
kisses my mouth, where we two are twice as long,
outstretched arms on hands [   ]
works his will   [   ]
[   ] filled that I come forth
[   ]
I cannot conceal the [   ]
[   ] in daylight
[   ]
men are with sound [   ]
[   ] token-marked who [ ] me to [   ]
[   ] the man you two were riding.

RIDDLE 97

Once he was alone and worked alone,
read alone, and cooked and ate alone
a red supper, a red celebration,
for when you are cut loose, drifting
as he was, not even trailing strings
behind, it's necessary, sometimes,
to tie down to something central,
embodied, hot. A steak, skillet-
seared, bloody. A bunch of beets
roasted, green tops torn off.
A bottle of wine, garnet-dark.

That was all.
                              Except to say
he ate in a cave by a pit of dragon-
scale coals. The stone hole glowed.
The coals spat sparks in their ash bed.
The shadows sung softly, susurrant.
They might have been dancing
but were not, only made a sound
which entered him like dance
until he dug in the coals with a branch
then tossed the branch on their backs.
If wispily it smoked through its leaves,
                              who, then, flamed?

WULF AND EADWACER

[translated from the Old English]

To my people   it is like a battle gift
They will consume him   in violence if he comes

We are unalike

Wulf is on one island   I am on another
That island is fixed fast   cast about by fens
There are carnage-covered   men on that island
They will consume him   in violence if he comes

We are unalike

My mind suffered   woe at Wulf's wanderings
When it was rainy weather   I sat and wept
When the battle-bold one   held me in his branches
There was joy in that   but it was hateful to me too

Wulf   my Wulf   it is not starvation but
my hopes for you   have made me sick
My mind mourns   your seldom-coming

Do you hear Eadwacer?   Wulf bears our
wretched   whelp to the wood
One easily cuts that   which was never joined
The tale of us two   together

DEAR LENGTHENING DAY

Come, swim under
       bitterness, seamstress.
We are two suspended
       up in the wet. Milky crestings, fringed
bare trees
       our only bulb to fend off rain.

How red the fire reeks below.
       Ocean and all its fiery ships
lapping, lapping at your dead feet,
       and my limbs are light-freighted and I am lapped in flame,
loose-jointed and afraid of nothing,
       wind-whetted, white-throated.
What seems most ourselves sinks to jet.

If the throb in the thin shell is real
       and fishblood denser than our blood,
you must not go alone into that place.
       We do not live among them.
They overlap, they tongue to tongue,
       they keep what is sharpest to themselves,
the bone that has no marrow
       gathered in a cold mouth.

Later, the snow came, and I
       had a change of temper.
Soon shall be the cough of birds,
       the deep dead wave,
wounds in the rain.

Let the night be drained.
       I am the scalp of myself.
I know it. But don't look at me.
       Forgive me
a bliss, a lightning blood.
       It was rainy weather and I wept by the hearth.

WHAT IS NIGHT

What is riven to its river
is it an edge jutting into darkness
what is darkness
night is darkness

I woke up in the weak-dark
there was blood everywhere
you had not come
night was a mesh
time ran streaming through

we used to say thee and also
thou which now looks like a half
word, like half of thought
we said it not for any you but
only the one without whom
I breaks

I broke the glass, was afraid to tell you.
What is better—hide the shards
display the glass's absence, or
gather evidence of a small localized
earthquake. That will never work.
When I think too much I fail.
Also when I don't think.

When like night nothing can stop my body
and it comes across the land,
a swathe of darkness it muscles down
across the stones and road and rows of wheat
and no oceans or army can stop my
out-flung cloak.

WORDS WERE CHANGING

Thanked for kindness, I said
you're welcome and welcome
spun back to what it meant,
before. Welcome, come
in, in accord with my will.
Come into warmth, you
are wanted, were waited
for. Welcome to these
arms, spread out, exposing
the bearer's heart.
You are well come, it is well
you have come for me.
    And if night swallows
us, it will be well, we
will be welcome—
the gates swing wide,
the bridge arcs tenderly
up over the river.
I laid a path, pruned
trees for your body
to pass through.
My bread, your bread.
My rafters, yours, timber
above our heads, or
to float on.

I fell asleep by the fire
near a bag of barley,
sweet smoke, and the kettle's
belly, rounded iron
forged on a day no sharpness
cut the mind of its maker.

There were other days
for sharpness, edges.
It is important to know
the difference of days,
and this was not one.

THE UNSTILL ONES

Since time unstrung
it had been happening
was always already going to
unbuckle its boots
and lace them back up.
That's what I call
a lace-buckle.

You ever are, you had been
ice that could vaporize
before watering. You come
in stages, often vapor
a chill mist of enveloping irises
each pistil sharpening
and I your whetstone, and
you will stone yourself
against my body

always now even before
but it is now again and
we were is-ing all over.
I didn't even have time
to explain how it
can happen when your
irises would freeze in the
midst of shifting

or how it could be
if past-ly my body was
blood-heavy and you are
not the mist then at all

nothing like mist. This is
how we will keep it heated
in the long night folded
back-outward.

BODY WALKING THROUGH SNOW

Begins as the body of a moving tree, greenwet
vines running up the trunk to the sun.
Crush of ice in the gutter, still street,
snow falling faithfully without sign of scarcity,
neverending driven flakes, yellow, yellow,
yellow-paint fire hydrant all but covered in slush,
head poked up, eager as a crocus.
Crust uneven underfoot: some people shoveled,
some did not shovel, one abandoned their shovel
in the hard hill's rind.
      Last night the moon was full,
now the moon is gone a gray flame,
pale light on last month's snow
under last week's snow under last night's snow
under more falling, and plows and shovels
make mazes, walls stacking fortresslike.
      Downhill, the body moves as water
coursing, burns star-blood,
breathes the un-seeable oxygen, breathes
in snow, out snow, in color, out color,
unbroken, supple. The body gives.
Eats the sorrow oranges growing here,
whose acid bite shocks the body
into blooming, forced as a bulb.
      Not silent, the snow air, there
is singing in it, bright as a throatful of juice
squeezed by a person in love who tended
in love the torsos of trees, and sang
alone on the road in the snow, unlost
in the parapets, unfrozen against the lake.
      I wonder why they don't
open their doors, slide

back the bolts to hear, to see this spectacle
flowering against the winter,
the body which became my body,
running in such wholeness that whichever
way I go is the way I go, body a blaze
of sudden cohesion,
word of words, song of songs.
This is how it happens. This is how.

RIDDLE 94

[translated from the Old English]

Smoother, [   ]
higher than heaven [   ]
[   ] gladder than the sun
[   ] [   ] steel,
sharper than salty [   ]
more beloved than all this light, lighter now [   ]

VOYAGES

"And could they hear me I would tell them:"

—Hart Crane

1.

What my mother and father,
body together with body,
made, I can not. Can jet
no living material. Too
private, too lowly to write?
Rain into the ocean today,
queer yellow light dropping
copper liquid into liquid.
Lightning: the jagging
rip of torn ozone, fan
gusting rain into the room,
lapping at the window box.

2.

We make fields of ourselves
we make rivers of ourselves
we geode in the bluejack oaks
we lay down what makes us heavy
we examine each thing until
we are naked, I mean
we are husked of heaviness,
we zero it out in Queen Anne's lace,
we inflow along the axis.

3.

Who would find a way
into your body from this motion?
Who sink in and root, quilt-grass

morning-built, ajar as a song
vaulting from a passing ship,
drawn by distant human music?
How ordinary this day is,
gauzy sift of clouds, spill of wax on wood,
whorl of an old knot grown smooth
from sand and polish, from stain,
oil from our hands, how
ordinary, to want this.

4.

White blossoms of the galax,
June vaulted spikes in the woods,
the sun, the high golden yolk,
black scent of soil. If what
comes from me is not life, it is
also not not life. Let me not
be questionless. Let me be
open as a vowel, wave-glazed.

5.

We lay on our backs and watched clouds
puff white over the sea. The clouds
so unsubtle: a rabbit, huge-haunched,
and snacking; a snow-fox, with pale
fur feathers. Then these kids clanked by,
buckets of brine, inexorably trotting
back and forth, ocean to the hole
they dug near their towels, galvanized
as their pails to this project of transfer,
bent to their trowels, squinting in the sun,
building a pool, a tiny ocean so close
to the ocean. What drives their feet,
hunched shoulders, to create this copy,
as a bundle of cloud shifts into the shape
of a gull? And already the living gulls,
which could be called real gulls,
if a person wanted to be petty,
which we did not, coasted through us.

RIDDLE 78

[translated from the Old English]

Often I [   ] floods [   ]
[   ] a kind of [   ] minnows
and [   ]
[   ] me to [   ]
[   ] as I to him [   ]
[   ] not at home sat
[   ] the deep sea killed
through skill-work [   ] bent on the brim of the sea

BREAKWATER

The snow was melting and the night
        smelled of just-tanned leather. Rock-
            salt in the streets, chemicals, sand,
    black slicks of ice. This was after the world
ended and began again. I thought everyone's
    heart had burned to ash.
            I woke up. It was winter, just like before.
    In New England, every house with a chimney
            chugged out smoke. The washer upstairs
    shook my bed. I thought it was music at first,
neighbors stomping, dancing. It was just a washer,
        unsteady, but spinning. Rocking on its stubby feet,
not at all like the earth turning.

Or exactly like that.
    I was wrong to think stars
more holy than soap, water, a force
    strong enough to wring dirt from socks.
I languished in traffic; you bought me a scotch.
    We walked to the sea and the night
        opened without metaphor, just ceased
    to be stone, turned porous.
The ships on the horizon: just ships
    hauling freight, or human passengers.
        And I became a human passenger again,
    weak at the water, waves breaking foam over snow.

Acknowledgments

I am extremely grateful to the editors of the following journals, in which some of these poems and translations have appeared, sometimes in variant forms: *14 Hills, Beloit Poetry Journal, berfrois, Boston Review, Gramma, Harvard Review Online, London Review of Books, the minnesota review, The Nation, Poetry, Southeast Review,* and *Tin House.*

I could not have made this book without the support of the Poetry Foundation, the 92nd Street Y, the Ledbury Poetry Festival, and the English Department at the University of Connecticut. To all my friends in Medieval Studies at UConn: thank you for the key to your library, both literal and figurative.

Many thanks to Susan Stewart for taking a chance on this book, and to Jodi Beder, Ellen Foos, Thalia Leaf, and Jodi Price at PUP for all their hard work, and to Jeanette Sears for the excellent photos.

I am forever grateful to my teachers and mentors: Maria Bell, Margaret Sönser Breen, Darcie Dennigan, Elizabeth Freeman, Alice Friman, Suzanne Gardinier, Marie Howe, Martin Lammon, Joan Larkin, Laura Newbern, Victoria Redel, and John Watkins; Robert Hasenfratz, who so patiently taught me to read and speak Old English; and V. Penelope Pelizzon, who has read these poems more times than I can count. In memory of Thomas Lux, the first person I ever met who loved poetry as much as I did, and who taught me how to "make the thing."

This has been years in the making, and I'm incredibly grateful for the friends and family who have offered me support, readership, and worldly sustenance: Ari Banias, Ana Božičević, Marcy Coburn, Owen Colás, Matthew Dickman, Bekah Dickstein, Sean Frederick Forbes, Micah Goodrich, Gísli Rúnar Harðarson, Trudie Kaiser, Nathan Levitt, Conrad Lumm, Jonas Moody, Jesse Oberman, Michael Rosen-Pyros, Leah Schwebel, Nicole Solomon, Jennifer Stanton DiLorenzo, Sara Jane Stoner, Julia Tillinghast, and Jarred Wiehe. To Eli and Susan Oberman, who are elemental; and in memory of so many, but especially Mark Oberman, Mary Rosen-Pyros, and Myron Rogers, who was rootin' for me.

For Louisa, *beshert* and *wyrd,* and for Rosa Sher, who is new.

Notes

Many of the translations in this book are taken from the *Exeter Book,* Exeter Cathedral Library MS 3501. This tenth-century codex is described by Ann Barwood, Canon Librarian, and Peter Thomas, Cathedral Librarian, as being "written in darkish brown ink and in a hand of fine character." In 2016 the *Exeter Book* was listed as one of the "world's principal cultural artefacts" by UNESCO, who consider it the "foundation volume of English literature." While at times I consulted a facsimile edition of the *Exeter Book,* most of these translations rely on George P. Krapp and Elliott V. K. Dobbie, *The Exeter Book* (Anglo-Saxon Poetic Records 3, New York: Columbia University Press, 1936).

"Night Watch" refers to "the un-still ones," a phrase borrowed from the definition, in "The Old English Rune Poem," of the runic character ᛖ, or "war horse," the nineteenth of 29 Anglo-Saxon runes.

"Cædmon's Hymn" dates to at least as early as the eighth century, and is sometimes considered the first poem written in English. In stark contrast to most Old English poetry, there were at least 21 medieval copies, and the one I use here is the West Saxon version from Elliot V.K. Dobbie's *Anglo-Saxon Minor Poems* (Anglo-Saxon Poetic Records VI). Whether or not you believe the Venerable Bede's story that the narrator, Cædmon, was an unlettered herdsman suddenly moved to poetry by divine intervention is up to you.

In three instances I have both translated and reacted to Old English poems, with the pair of poems bearing the same title. One such case is "Wulf and Eadwacer." The lone surviving copy of the original "Wulf and Eadwacer" sits on folio 100v of the *Exeter Book.* Nineteen lines long, it is, with "The Wife's Lament," one of only a few Old English poems that are arguably written in the voice of a woman (made evident in the poem by the adjectives "reotugu," the grammatically feminine word for "mournful," in line 10, and "seoce," the feminine form for "sick," in line 14). The poem is generally considered an elegy, although arguments have been made that it is a riddle, a charm, a funeral lament, or a story about wolves. The poem involves, probably, a woman, at least two men (although some say one man, some say more), and a child. It's nearly impossible to find any discussion of this poem without reference to Benjamin Thorpe's comment in

1842—after attempting to transcribe, annotate, and translate the poem, Thorpe declared, "Of this I can make no sense."

"Aloud, Out of Nothing" and "Dear Lengthening Day" are shortened centos, poems composed entirely of lines borrowed from other works. These include lines from (in no particular order) anonymous medieval poems (translated by Michael J. Alexander), H.D., Isaac McLellan, Robert Herrick, Alfred Tennyson, Abbie Houston Evans, Robert Hayden, Edwin Markham, John Berryman, Harry Brown, George Herbert, Andrew Marvell, Tomas Tranströmer, Kenneth Rexroth (translating from the Greek), Emily Dickinson, Stephen Crane, Denise Levertov, Virgil, Carolyn Stoloff, Edward Dorn, Larissa Szporluk, Cole Swenson, Richard Tillinghast, Susan Stewart, James Wright, and Joan Swift.

"The Ruin" is translated from folio 8 of the *Exeter Book*. While generally well preserved, the *Exeter Book* is severely damaged in several places and appears to have been used as both a cutting board and a beer coaster. The last 14 folios are scarred by a long, diagonal burn, damage likely caused by a hot poker, and "The Ruin" is missing around 14 half lines; in this and other translations from Old English, missing text is indicated by brackets.

I borrowed the titles for "Tabula Rasa" and "Silentium" from Arvo Pärt's double concerto *Tabula Rasa*.

"The Woman Who Cannot" is a translation of an Old English metrical charm, variants of which can be found in *Bald's Leechbook*, compiled in the ninth century and sometimes called "Medicinale Anglicum," and *The Lacnunga*, a slightly later medical compendium (British Library MS Harley 585).

Riddles 82, 63, 94, and 78 can all be found in a severely burned section of the *Exeter Book*; "Riddle 97" cannot.

There is no surviving medieval copy of "The Old English Rune Poem." The only known copy of the "Rune Poem" was in Cotton MS Otho B.X, folio 165. In 1731, the Cottonian Library was moved to Ashburnham House, which was devastated by fire in that same year (the name of the house itself suggesting it may not have been the best place to keep flammable items). Luckily, a handwritten copy had been made early in the eighteenth century. This copy also was lost (to a different fire), but not before it was copied by George Hickes, who published a print edition in 1705 in his *Linguarum Veterum Septentrionalium Thesaurus*. The edition I worked from is Elliot V.K. Dobbie's *Anglo-Saxon Minor Poems*. The sound in the last stanza (defining the rune for "earth," in this case used to depict a grave) of the "Rune Poem" suffers particularly in translation, and I will sleep better for reproducing it in Old English here:

(Ear) byþ egle eorla gehwylcun,
ðonn[e] fæstlice flæsc onginneþ,
hraw colian, hrusan ceosan
blac to gebeddan; bleda gedreosaþ,
wynna gewitaþ, wera geswicaþ.

"The Grave," found on folio 170r of MS Bodley 343, is a translation of what is thought to be the last poem written in Old English. The last three lines were added on later, in Middle English, by a scribe medievalists refer to as "the tremulous hand of Worcester."

"Against a Sudden Stitch" and "Against a Dwarf" are translated from Elliot V.K. Dobbie's *Anglo-Saxon Minor Poems*.

Princeton Series of Contemporary Poets